PRETTY IN PINK

WHY IT'S GOOD TO BE A GIRL!

PRETTY IN PINK

WHY IT'S GOOD TO BE A GIRL!

Bob Elsdale and Vasilisa

Andrews McMeel
Publishing, LLC

Kansas City

In this modern world **it's good to be a girl.**

We have the looks, the style, and the freedom to do what we want—whenever we want to do it. The world is our oyster and it can be shucked whenever we choose.

So it's hard to imagine this wasn't always the case.

There was once a time when we girls had a hard time getting a fair deal. Oh, it was all very well that we were shaped from sugar and spice and all things nice but when the folks in charge were the ones constructed from slugs, snails, and puppy-dog tails, it was a bit too easy to be ignored.

We found ourselves shoved into home economics classes or secretarial jobs, expected to spend our days deciding who we'd want to marry or what to name our first offspring. Boys just didn't seem to want to share. They thought opening doors and picking up the tab at dinner was going to keep us satisfied.

We tried to warn them.

We dropped hints about perhaps being interested in more than cooking and babies. We suggested that we might be able to manage the company with a touch more attention to detail than they could. But the boys would just give us a roll of the eyes and a condescending pat on the knee before sidling off to watch the game with their puppy-dog pals. Something had to snap.

From the first whiff of smoldering bra strap they should have seen it coming, but by the time the boys realized they were in trouble the bonfire was stoked with enough underwire support to become the inferno that changed the gender landscape forever.

It was the dawning of the age of Girl Power.

These days we're the ones buying the dinner, and the boys who open doors for us are usually looking for a tip. You are just as likely to see a pair of Manolos beneath the CEO's desk as a pair of brogues and we girls judge our prospective partners by their diaper-changing skills rather than the size of their salary.

Having proved our point, shopping is now our sport and the boutiques of the world our playing field. And the poor boys struggle to be like *us*!

Yes, it's good to be a girl . . . but it's even better to be two. Or three. Or four.

Nothing on earth can brighten your outlook quicker than a few minutes, hours, or days spent with a girlfriend. Whether it's a quick chat on the phone, a snatched coffee between appointments, a night at the movies, or a weekend spent hiking in the mountains, there's beauty in numbers.

It's the girls who are pretty in pink (and I certainly wouldn't tell you otherwise).

❧ IT'S GOOD TO

BE A GIRL. ❧

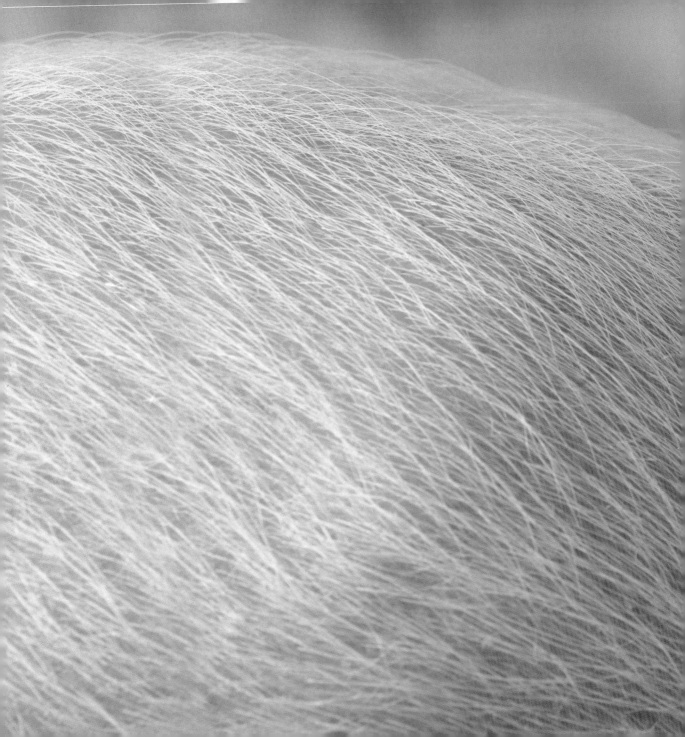

SO GIVE LIFE

A TWIRL!

THE WORLD IS
OUR OYSTER,

AND EVERYTHING IS COMING UP ROSES.

WE GIRLS HAVE SO MANY

FABULOUS FACETS.

SO FOLLOW YOUR DREAMS,

THE SKY'S THE LIMIT.

GIRLS CAN DO

ANYTHING BOYS CAN . . .

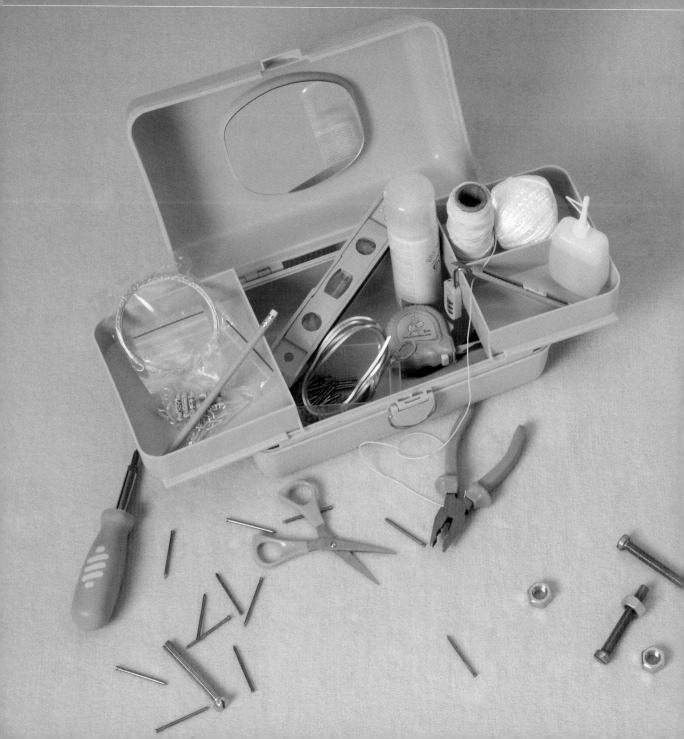

JUST WITH
CONSIDERABLY

MORE STYLE.

EVERY DAY IS A

SPECIAL DAY.

BUT WHEN LIFE

GETS YOU DOWN,

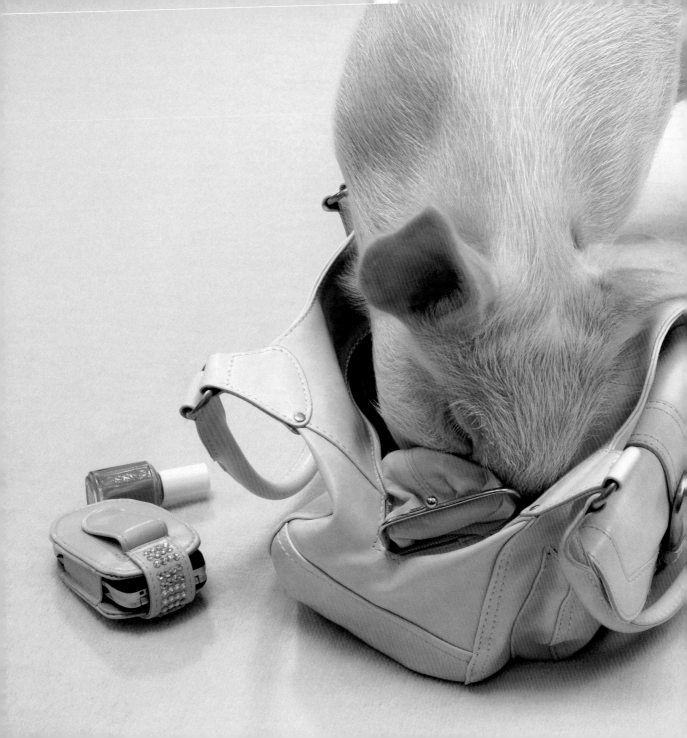

OR YOU JUST CAN'T
FIND WHAT YOU'RE
LOOKING FOR,

IT'S IMPORTANT TO FIND TIME . . .

FOR LIFE'S LITTLE ESSENTIALS . . .

LIKE RETAIL

THERAPY,

AND THE PURSUIT OF THE

PERFECT PAIR . . .

TO COMPLEMENT THE PERFECT OUTFIT.

PARTYING IS BEST OF ALL.

[GIRLS NEVER NEED AN EXCUSE FOR THAT!]

BUT SOMETIMES . . .

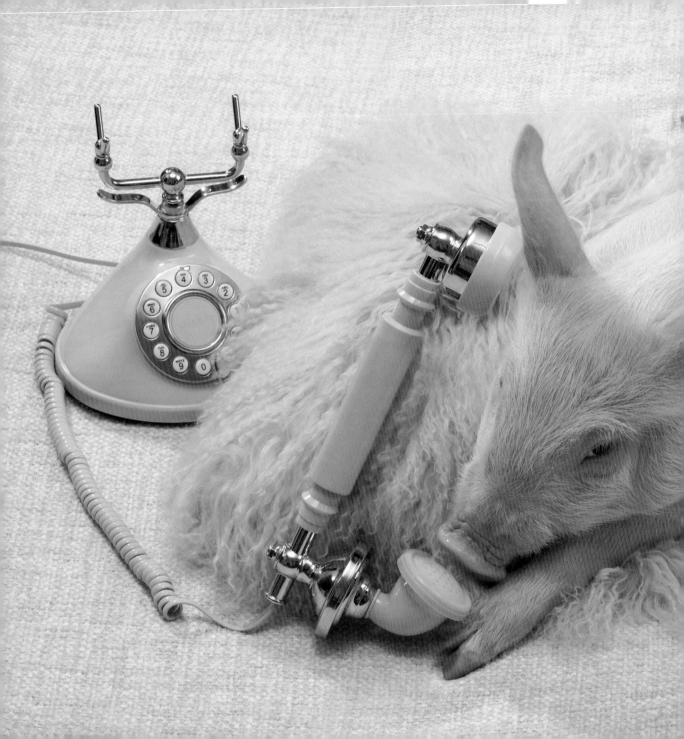

IT'S NICE TO HAVE

A NIGHT IN.

OR JUST TO CATCH UP ON YOUR

BEAUTY SLEEP.

DAILY MAINTENANCE CAN BE FUN.

BUT PAMPERING YOURSELF . . .

_____ ❧ _____

IS ONE OF LIFE'S JOYS.

❧

YOU CAN ALWAYS WORK IT OFF THE NEXT DAY.

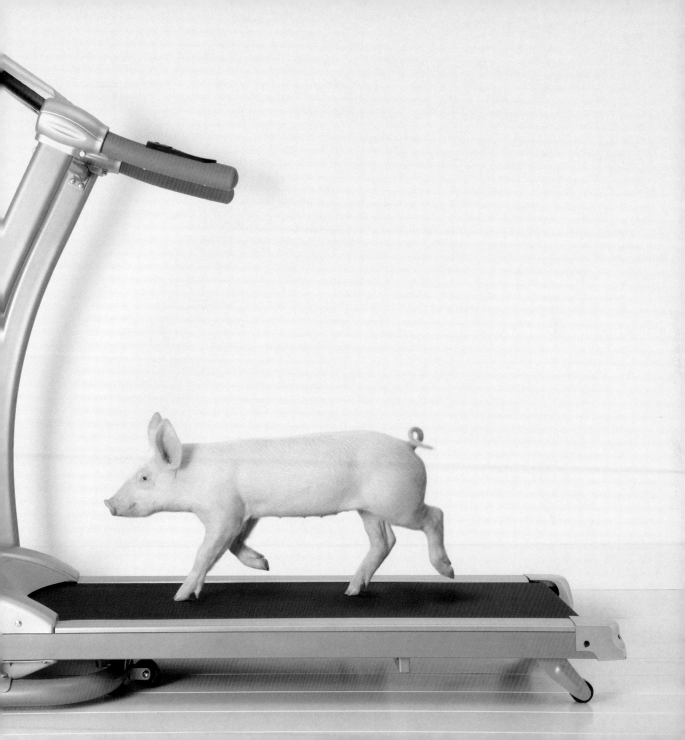

AND IF THINGS GET

OUT OF BALANCE . . .

THERE'S ALWAYS SELF-DELUSION.

AND WHEN YOU'VE
HAD TOO MUCH OF A

GOOD THING . . .

 OR

EVEN BETTER . . . ✤

TO CATCH UP WITH

THE GIRLS.

AND CURRENT AFFAIRS!

❧ THE WORLD IS TRULY OUR

OYSTER, AND REMEMBER . . . ❧

SOMETIMES OUR
BEST ASSETS ARE

BEHIND US.

[THE END]

NO PIGS WERE HARMED IN THE MAKING OF THIS BOOK.

Having already worked with pigs on an advertising campaign in the UK I knew they would be challenging subjects! But, apart from their ability to make more noise than a siren, they are also universally loved. Pigs are woven into so many childhood tales and rhymes; they are also highly intelligent, cute, and pink. The obvious way to tackle this book was to raise our own animals and work with their individual personalities.

However, pigs don't really have expressive faces except when chewing and eating (something they are internally programmed to do a lot of). The use of high-speed flash coupled with lots of patience and understanding proved a powerful combination in getting the pigs to pose as we wished. Most animals respond well to rewards, which in a pig's case is either cheese or grapes. Getting one to run on a treadmill was just a matter of timing, cheese, and slowly turning up the power! Flash, click . . . job done.

The time it took to create each image varied, but in general the images took at least a day each. Sometimes the pig had to be trained to do a specific task so of course it took a lot longer. Sometimes, but not often, we had to repeat the photography maybe two or three times until we achieved the look we all wanted. Talented as the pigs were, enthusiastic and intelligent as they might be, I can't attribute any of the art direction to them. The concepts behind the pictures were all ours. But maybe George Orwell knew something about pigs we don't when he wrote the superb book *Animal Farm*!

I work closely with my assistants, whom I recruit for their creative and imaginative skills. Just as important is the requirement to allow the animal to become part of your family. We had two piglets—Rosie and Petal—one after the other, and both needed night feeds for the first week. These projects are very much a team effort and require huge amounts of patience and dedication from all concerned.

Rosie and Petal had completely different personalities. My wife bought a pink pig harness and Rosie went for a walk every day with our three dogs. She was a very laid-back character who developed a passion for trying to nose up chewing gum from the pavement. Her other great love was mango stones, which she would suck on for a very long time.

Petal, on the other hand, was much more aloof and at times quite petulant. If she wasn't in the mood to work with us we quickly learned to take a tea break and start again.

Corn on the cob was one treat that would last a long time. Trying to peel them with trotters did take a while. On more than one occasion we had to unblock our drains, which is where they pushed the cobs when finished.

We had to pay special attention to the pigs' skincare as their skin burns very easily. Left to their own devices they use mud as protection. If you want a pig to stay pink rather than bright red, SPF 50 is the order of the day.

Pigs need pig time so at least half our daffodil bulbs were routed out and eaten, which was no big deal. However, finding bedding plants pulled up just for fun was taxing at times. Needless to say when you needed a clean pig it was usually to be found in the garden up to its eyebrows in dirt!

It is good to know that the pigs' working lives were particularly short and that they are now both enjoying early retirement together on Bocketts Farm, Leatherhead, Surrey, UK. When we last visited them it was quite clear that their time with us was not even a distant memory. This, coupled with the fact that they will never become sausages, is just the way it should be.

Bob Elsdale

ACKNOWLEDGMENTS

I would like to thank the following people for making this book possible.

My wife, Christine, for happily doing the multiplicity of tasks required to look after the needs of juvenile pigs: from administering sunscreen (to prevent them going a little too pink in the sun) to mentoring and training them to satisfying their ceaseless obsession for food, and so many other things that I have forgotten and probably took for granted.

To my assistant, Vasilisa, for coming up with a number of the concepts for the images, and for her excellent styling skills for all things pink in color.

To my family members Louise and Elizabeth at Oathill Farm for supplying the pigs. Somehow Louise can determine the future character of a pig from its body language and attitude at only a few days old. She was not wrong.

To Bocketts Farm for taking Rosie and Petal and providing them with a retirement home for life.

This edition published by Andrews McMeel Publishing, LLC, an Andrews McMeel Universal company, 4520 Main Street, Kansas City, Missouri 64111.

ISBN-13: 978-0-7407-6910-8
ISBN-10: 0-7407-6910-3

Library of Congress Control Number: 2007923204

Produced and originated by PQ Blackwell Limited
116 Symonds Street, Auckland, New Zealand
www.pqblackwell.com

Book concept, photography, and digital art Bob Elsdale and Vasilisa

Thanks to Sarah-Kate Lynch and Rob Cassels for their contribution to the text.

www.andrewsmcmeel.com

Artwork design by Carolyn Lewis

Printed by Everbest Printing International Ltd., China